THEATRE, WITH FOOTLIGHTS.

The best Miniature Toy Theatre in the market. Strongly made and fitted with properly working curtain, English pattern, footlights to burn oil, beautifully lithographed characters, mounted on cardboard and cut ready for use. These Theatres have complete set of characters, etc., as per book.

No.	2a	3a	5a	8a
	7/11	13/9	18/6	37/6

Postage 6d. under 20/- in value.

ZILLOGRAPH or SHADOW THEATRE.
Price ... 6d. and 10½d.   Post 2d. and 3d.

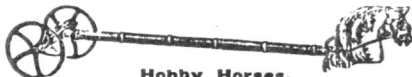

With Six Notes and changeable pictures.

Price .. .. 6d.   Post 2d.

The Vocophone.

An Evening's Entertainment in your Waistcoat Pocket.

Try this simple MUSICAL NOVELTY. It will strengthen your Voice, and develop true sounds.

You can imitate all Brass Instruments, rendering good Solos.

The effect of harmonizing is good. It is a companion to the Cyclist and Scout. The Vocophone will do anything you wish it to do, as regards intensifying vocal sounds. By removing the cap and speaking through the tube, it will increase the sound given forth, and will answer the purpose of a **Pocket Megaphone.**

Price, with instructions, 6d.   Post 1d.

Hobby Horses.

No. 1B .. 2/9   No. 2B .. 3/6

AN EARLY PERFORMANCE IN COVENT GARDEN

PUNCH & JUDY

FROM
THE WORKS OF
PAYNE COLLIER
ILLUSTRATED BY
GEORGE CRUIKSHANK
WITH ADDITIONAL MATERIAL FROM THE 19TH CENTURY
REVISED & COMPILED BY
MICHAEL D. EVERETT
M·D·E PUBLICATIONS

Published by

(mde)

MDE PUBLICATIONS
16 Hardwick Crescent
Sheffield S11 8WB
Tel: 0742 665136
Restoration & Design
© Michael D. Everett 1993
ISBN 0 906933 70-6
Printed in England by
MDE PRINT UNIT
Designed & Typeset by
MDE PUBLICATIONS

ACKNOWLEDGEMENTS

The publishers wish to thank
Peter Baldwin for supplying
the original source material
from his collection without
which this book could not have
been produced. Also the
Benjamin Pollock Toy Shop of
Covent Garden, London for
their encouragement when
compiling this book.

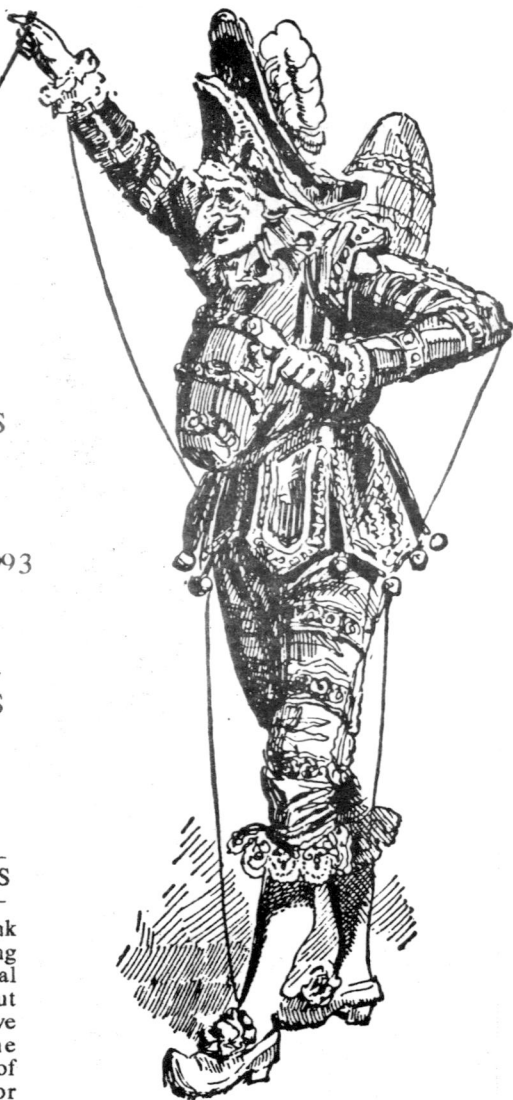

STAGE-STRUCK

Stage-struck! stage-struck! What is that!"
Hear, and I will tell you what :-
It is to run stark mad for plays;
To waste your nights and spend your days
In studying how to make a face
With true theatrical grimace;
'Tis how to manufacture groans,
And sing in sickening semi-tones;
It is the mouth to screw and pinch,
Whilst killing Shakespear inch by inch;
It is to think yourself a king,
A beggar, knave, or any thing;
It is to dress just like a fool,
And run away from work or school;
To be the public's laughing-stock,
And sometimes even virtue mock;
At all events, not to be nice
In gilding o'er some pleasing vice.
These, with some exceptions, rare,
Are stage-struck features, I declare.

*from The Half-Holiday Task Book,
Printed by Hodgeson and Co, Juvenile
Press, Newgate St., London c.1820
(Bradley Toy Theatre Collection)*

PUNCH'S
THEATRICAL
TOURING
COMPANY

FANTOCCINI PERFORMS IN LONDON'S EAST END

FANTOCCINI

In the simulative theatricals of the streets, the Fantoccini, when they existed, might be considered as the legitimate drama; Punch as sensational melodrama. The Punch puppets, as is well known - but what a pity it should be known! - are managed by an unseen performer below the stage, who has his fingers thrust up within their dresses, so as to move the head and arms only. In the case of the Fantoccini, all the figures have movable joints, governed by a string, and managed by a man who stands behind the scene, passing his arms above the stage, and so regulating the actions of his dramatic personae. The Fantoccini were in considerable vogue in the bye streets of London in the reign of George IV, on the limited scale represented by our artist. Turks, sailors, clowns etc. dangled and danced through the scene with great propriety of demeanour, much to the delight of the young and the gaping wonderment of strangers.

Few persons who gazed upon the grotesque movements of these figures imagined the profound age of their invention. The Fantoccini introduced as a novelty within our own remembrance, in reality had its chief features developed in the days of the Pharaohs; for in the tombs of ancient Egypt, figures have been found whose limbs were made movable for the delight of children before Moses was born. In the tombs of Etruria similar toys have been discovered; they were disseminated in the East; and in China and India are now made to act dramas, either as movable figures or as shows behind a curtain. As 'ombres Chinoises' these figures made a novelty for London sightseers at the end of the 18th century; and may still be seen on winter nights in London performing a brief, grotesque, and not over-delicate drama, originally produced at Astley's Ampitheatre, and there known as "The Broken Bridge".

It requires considerable dexterity to 'work' these figures well; and when several are grouped together, the labour is very great, requiring quick hand and steady eye. The exhibition does not 'pay' now so well as Punch; because it is too purely mechanical, and lacks the bustle and fun, the rough practical joking and comicality of that great original creation. The proprietors of these shows complain of this degenerate taste; but it is as possible for the manager of a street show to be in advance of the taste of his audience as for the manager of a Theatre Royal; and the 'sensation dramas' now demanded by the theatre-goers, are to better plays what Punch is to the Fantoccini.

INTRODUCTION

It is probably safe to say that there is no boy or girl in the country who has not a t some time or other seen a performance of Punch and Judy. Mr. Punch's performances are familiar to all ages, and yet very few if asked the question, could tell how long such exhibitions have been common in England, or when the story of "Punch and Judy" was first invented and exhibited. Strange to say, with one exception, no attempt has been made by those people who write books to illustrate the origin, biography, and character of a person so notorious as Mr. Punch.

There was however, one man named Payne Collier (1789-1883) who about one-hundred and eighty years ago, took the trouble to write such a history and with assistance of his friend George Cruikshank (1792-1878) published a book telling all that there was to tell about Punch and Judy. George Cruikshank made a lot of drawings illustrating the performance from beginning to end. This publication is an edited version of that book.

The fame of Mr. Punch has spread all over the civilised world; but he was first invented in Italy. His original name was probably Pulcinella, and he first came into existence at Acerra, and ancient city only a short distance from Naples and Mount Vesuvius. The man who invented the Italian Punch, or Pulcinella, was called Silvio Fiorillo, and he lived about four-hundred years ago, at a time when it was the custom in Italy for public comedians or comic actors to travel about the country giving private performances of a light and laughable character - quite different from those more serious performances given in colleges and private houses of the wealthy by the greater actors and reciters of that time. These travelling entertainers usually performed very foolish plays or fables, in which the words spoken were not carefully written out and committed to memory beforehand, but the dialogue was left very much to the free will of the performers, who made it up as they went along. They were, however, extremely popular among the poorer classes throughout Italy, and Silvio Fiorillo probably invented his story of Punch as a new entertainment for the strolling players of Naples.

At that time Mr. Punch was no doubt one of the living performers, but after a while he ceased to be anything more than a mere puppet or doll in what many years ago were called puppet shows, and were popular in our own country. We do not know whether Mr. Punch became a mere puppet before or after he left the land of his birth,

A VICTORIAN STREET SCENE

but probably it was before his performances became known in countries other than Italy. However that may be, puppet shows are of a very ancient date in England. They were sometimes called also "motion" plays, because the puppets or dolls were dressed as nearly as possible like the actors in real plays, and the dolls were worked by means of wires by the man who owned the show. Sometimes the puppet play was accompanied by a dialogue: that is to say, the dolls were supposed to talk to each other, as in the Punch and Judy of today: and in others the dolls were only set in motion for the amusement of the spectators, without any talking at all.

The most ancient puppet shows were representations of stories taken from the Bible, or from the lives and legends of the Saints; but towards the end of the reign of Elizabeth, historical and other fables began to be exhibited by the puppet showman. The Bible stories, however, were the more popular, especially those of the Prodigal Son, Jonah and the Whale, the Story of the Flood and the Building of Solomon's Temple. Fleet-street and Holborn Bridge being the favourite thoroughfares in which to set up exhibitions. The shows generally consisted of a wretched display of wooden figures, badly formed and decorated, and without the least degree of taste or propriety. The wires with which they were made to move could be seen at the top of their heads, and the dialogues were mere jumbles of absurdities and nonsense. When the 19th century opened, the performances of Punch and Judy were less objectionable than in earlier days; but, nevertheless, they were still too coarse to be reproduced exactly in this book, for in those days people were not so educated as they are today, and it was customary for men and women in all classes of society to talk in a way which would shock respectable people these days.

Mr. Punch seems to have arrived in England something like 300 years ago. The first great exhibitor of the shows was a certain Mr. Powell, who set up his show in Covent Garden, opposite to St. Paul's Church; and in an old newspaper dated 1711 there is a letter from the sexton of the church, who complained the performances of Mr. Punch thinned the congregation in St. Paul's Church, Covent Garden, and that as Mr. Powell exhibited his show during the times of prayers, the tolling of the church bell was taken by all who heard it for notice of the intended commencement of the exhibition. This reads very strange nowadays, but Mr. Powell seems to have mixed up many other favourite stories of the nursery with his history of Punch and Judy, for he often represented the tale of the Children in the Wood, Dick Whittington and his Cat, Robin Hood, Mother Shipton and Mother Goose. With such exhibitions the great showman is said to have "kept the churches empty." Certainly, at this time, Mr. Punch was held by the multitude in high favour. Some suppose that he came to England about the same time as King William. However that may be, we do not know that the dress and appearance of Punch in 1731 were as nearly as possible like what they are now.

We have no means of knowing with certainty what was the nature of the earliest exhibitions of Punch and his merry family, as the performances very much resemble the impromptu comedies of the Italians, and so no record exists of the dialogues. At various stages the adventures of Punch have been differently represented, and changes have been introduced to suit the taste of the audience and to meet the requirements of the time. For example, after the battle of the Nile, Lord Nelson frequently figured in the Punch and Judy performances, on which occasions the hero of the Nile was want to hold conversations with Mr. Punch in order to persuade him, as a brave fellow, to go on board his ship and help to fight the French. "Come Punch, my boy, " said the Naval hero, "I'll make you a captain or a commodore, if you like it." "But I don't like it," replied the puppet-show hero; "I shall be drowned." "Never fear that," answered Nelson; "he that is born to be hanged, you know, is sure not to be drowned."

The following text of the adventures of Mr. Punch has been taken from Mr. Cruikshank's book; but it has been carefully edited in order to avoid the too coarse language in which the performers indulged 170 years ago. The writer of the book in question founded his conversation chiefly upon the performance of an old Italian puppet-showman named Piccini, who had perambulated London and the country for fifty years. This man then lived in the district of Drury Lane. He had lost one eye, always wore an oilskin hat and a rough grey coat; on his back he carried a box containing the figures used in the show, and in his hand a trumpet, at the blast of which hundreds of merry little faces flocked round him with open mouths, all eager to renew their acquaintance with their old friend and favourite, Mr. Punch. Piccini's exhibition was the first given in the language of his own country, but by degrees he learned a little broken English, and adapted his show more to the taste of his English audiences; and you may have noticed that the performers of Punch and Judy who are natives of our own country generally try to imitate an outlandish dialect.

You must not suppose that the character of Mr. Punch is one to be imitated, for, as a matter of fact, his character left much to desired; but the show is not treated very seriously by those who go to see it. It is regarded rather as a joke, the most effective part of which is the ultimate triumph of the hero. In the course of the adventures Mr. Punch is guilty of ridiculous and extravagant conduct; but confidence and presence of mind are always useful, and these never deserted Mr. Punch; and when he was first carried around England, his exhibitors, no doubt, wished to show that his confidence and presence of mind, combined with his prudent courage, were sufficient to carry him through every difficulty and help him to triumph over every adversity.

MR PUNCH MOVES ON

PUNCH & JUDY

After a few preliminary squeaks, Punch bows three times to the spectators, once in the centre, and once at each side of the stage, and then squeaks the following:

PROLOGUE
Ladies and Gentlemen, pray how do you do?
If you're all happy, I'm all happy too.
Stop and hear my merry little play;
If I make you laugh, I need not make you pay.

Exit

ACT I
Punch is heard behind the scene squeaking some well-known tune; he then makes his appearance and dances about the stage, while he sings these lines:

Mr. Punch is one jolly good fellow,
His dress is all scarlet and yellow,
And if now and then he gets mellow,
It's only among his good friends.
His money most freely he spends;
To laugh and grow fat he intends;
'Tis true he's a rogue and a rover,
He lives, while he can, upon clover;
When he dies - why, then it's all over,
And there Punch's comedy ends.

He continues to dance and sing, and then calls "Judy, my dear! Judy". Enter the dog Toby.

PUNCH. Hullo, Toby! Who called you? How do you do Mr. Toby? I hope you are very well Mr. Toby.

TOBY. Bow, wow, wow!

PUNCH. How is my good friend, your master, Mr. Toby? How is Mr. Scaramouch?

TOBY. Bow, wow, wow!

PUNCH. I'm glad to hear it. Poor Toby! What a nice, good-tempered dog it is! No wonder his master is so fond of him.

TOBY. *(Snarls)* Arr! Arr!

PUNCH. What! Toby! You're very cross this morning. Did you get out of bed the wrong way upwards?

TOBY. *(Snarls again)* Arr! Arr!

PUNCH. Poor Toby! *(Putting his hand out cautiously and trying to coax the dog who snaps at it.)* Toby, you're one very nasty, cross dog - get away with you! *(Strikes at him)*

TOBY. Bow, wow, wow! *(Seizing Punch by the nose.)*

PUNCH. Oh, dear! Oh, dear! My nose! My poor nose! My beautiful nose! Get away! Get away, you nasty dog! I'll tell your master! Oh, dear, dear! - Judy, Judy!

Punch shakes his head, but cannot shake off the dog, who follows him as he retreats round the stage. He continues to call "Judy! Judy, my dear!" until the dog quits its hold and disappears.

PUNCH. (rubbing his nose with both hands) Oh, my nose! My pretty little nose! Judy! Judy! You nasty, nasty brute! I will tell your master of you! Mr. Scaramouch! My good friend, Scaramouch! Look what your nasty brute of a dog has done!

Enter Mr. Scaramouch with a stick.

SCARAMOUCH. Hullo! Mr. Punch. What have you been doing to my poor dog?

PUNCH. (retreating behind the side scene on observing the stick, and peeping round the corner) Ha! My good friend, how do you do? Glad to see you look so well *(aside)* I wish you were farther away with your nasty great stick.

SCARAMOUCH. Have you been beating and ill-using my poor dog, Mr. Punch.

PUNCH. He has been biting and ill-using my poor nose. What have you got there, sir?

SCARAMOUCH. Where?

PUNCH. In your hand.

SCARAMOUCH. A fiddle.

PUNCH. A fiddle! What a pretty thing is a fiddle! Can you play that fiddle.

SCARAMOUCH. Come here and I'll try.

PUNCH. No thank you, I can hear the music very well from here.

SCARAMOUCH. Then you shall try yourself. Can you play?

PUNCH. *(coming in)* I don't know till I try. Let me see. *(takes the stick and moves slowly about, singing a tune of which he is very fond. He hits Scaramouch a slight blow on his high cap, as if by accident.)*

SCARAMOUCH. You play very well Mr. Punch. Now let me try. I will give you a lesson how to play the fiddle. *(takes the stick and dances to the same tune, hitting Punch a hard blow on the back of the head.)* There's sweet music for you!

PUNCH. I don't like your playing so well as my own. Let me try again. *(takes stick and dances as before. In the course of his dance he gets behind Scaramouch and, with a violent blow, knocks his head clean off his shoulders.)* How do you like that tune, my good friend? That sweet music or sour music, eh? He! He! He! *(Laughing and throwing away the stick)* You'll never hear such another tune so long as you live, my boy. *(Sings the same tune again and dances to it)* Judy! Judy, my dear! Judy! Can't you answer my dear?

JUDY. *(within)* Well, what do you want, Mr. Punch?

PUNCH. Come upstairs; I want you.

JUDY. Then want must be your master. I'm busy.

PUNCH. (singing) -

Yet, why should I grumble and fret
Because she's sometimes in a pet?
Though I really am sorry to say, sirs,
That that is too often her way sirs,
For this, by and by, she shall pay, sirs.
Oh, wives are an obstinate set!

- Judy my dear! (calling) Judy, my love! Pretty Judy! Come upstairs!

JUDY. Well here I am! What do you want now I've come?

PUNCH. *(aside)* What a pretty creature! Isn't she a beauty?

JUDY. What do you want I say?

PUNCH. A kiss! A pretty kiss! *(he kisses her while she slaps him on the face)*

JUDY. Take that then. How do you like my kisses? Will you have another?

PUNCH. No; one at a time, one at a time, my sweet pretty wife. *(aside)* She always is so playful! Where's the baby? Fetch me the baby, judy, my dear. *(Exit Judy)*

PUNCH. *(to himself)* There's a wife for you! What a precious darling creature! She goes to fetch our child.

Re-enter Judy with the child.

JUDY. Here's the baby. Pretty dear! It knows its papa. Take the child.

PUNCH. *(holding out his hands)* Give it to me, pretty little thing! How like its sweet mamma!

JUDY. How awkward you are!

PUNCH. Give it to me; I know how to nurse it as well as you do. *(She gives it to him)* Get away!

Exit Judy

PUNCH. *(nursing the child in his arms)* What a pretty baby it is! Was it sleepy then? Hush-a-by-by. *(sings to the tune of* "Rest thee, baby")-

> Oh rest thee, my baby,
> Thy daddy is here:
> Thy mammy's a gaby,
> And that's very clear.
> Oh, rest thee, my darling,
> Thy mother will come,
> With a voice like a starling -
> I wish she was dumb!

Poor dear little thing! It cannot get to sleep! By-by-by-by, hush-a-by. Well, then, it sha'n't. *(Dances the child and then sets it upon his lap, between his knees, and sings the common nursery ditty):*

> Dancy baby diddy,
> What shall daddy do widdy?
> Sit on his lap,
> Give it some pap;
> Dance baby diddy.

After nursing it upon his lap, Punch sticks the child against the side of the stage on the platform and going himself to the opposite side, runs up to it, clapping his hands and crying, "catchee, catchee, catchee!" He then takes it up again and it begins to cry.

PUNCH. What is the matter with it?, Poor thing! It has got the stomach-ache, I dare say. *(Child cries)* Hush-a-by, hush-a-by! (Sitting down and rolling it on his knees) Naughty child! - Judy! *(Calling)* The child has got the stomach ache. Judy, I say! *(Child continues to cry)* Keep quiet, can't you? *(Hits it a box on the ear.)* Oh, you naughty child! What have you done? I won't keep such a naughty child! Hold your tongue! *(Strikes child's head several*

times against the side of the stage.) There! There! There! How do you like that? I thought I'd stopped your squalling. Get along with you, nasty, naughty, crying child! *(throws it off the front of the stage amongst spectators.)* He, he, he!

Re-enter Judy.

> *JUDY.* Where is the child?
> *PUNCH.* Gone - gone to sleep.
> *JUDY.* What have you done with the child I say?
> *PUNCH.* Gone to sleep, I say.
> *JUDY.* What have you done with it?
> *PUNCH.* What have I done with it?
> *JUDY.* Aye, done with it! I heard it crying just now. Where is

it!

> *PUNCH.* How should I know.
> *JUDY.* I heard you make the pretty darling cry.
> PUNCH. I dropped it out of the window.
> JUDY. Oh you cruel horrid wretch, to drop the pretty baby out of the window! Oh! (cries, and wipes her eyes with the corner of her white apron.) You wicked man! Oh, I'll make you pay for this depend upon it!

Exit in haste.

> *PUNCH.* There she goes. What a piece of work about nothing! *(Dances about and sings, beating time with his head, as he turns round, on the front of the stage.)*

Re-enter Judy with a stick. She comes in behind, and hits Punch a sounding blow on the back of his head before he is aware.

> *JUDY.* I'll teach you to drop the baby out of the window.
> *PUNCH.* Softly, Judy, softly! *(Rubbing the back of his head with his hand)* Don't be silly now. What are you at?
> *JUDY.* What! You'll drop my poor baby out of the window

again, will you? *(Hitting him over and over again on the head.)*

PUNCH. No, I never will again. *(she still hits him.)* Softly I say, softly! A joke's a joke!

JUDY. Oh you nasty cruel brute! *(Hitting him again)* I'll teach you!

PUNCH. But I don't like such teaching. What! You're in earnest are you?

JUDY. Yes *(whack!)* - I *(Whack!)* - am *(Whack!).*

PUNCH. I'm glad of it. I don't like such jokes. *(She hits him again)* Leave off, I say! What! You won't, will you?

JUDY. No, I won't! *(Hits him.)*

PUNCH. Very well; then now come's my turn to teach you. *(he struggles with Judy for the stick, which he presently wrenches from her, and strikes her with it on the head, while she runs about to different parts of the stage to get out of his way.)* How do you like my teaching, Judy, my pretty dear *(Hitting her.)*

JUDY. Oh, pray, Mr. Punch, no more!

PUNCH. Yes, one little more lesson. (hits her again.) There, there, there! *(She falls with her head over the platform of the stage, and he continues to hit at her. She puts up her hand to guard her head.)* Any more?

JUDY. No, no, no more! *(Lifting up her head.)*

PUNCH. *(Knocking down her head.)* I thought I should soon make you quiet.

JUDY. *(again raising her head.)* No.

PUNCH. *(again knocking it down.)* Now if you're satisfied, I am. *(Perceiving that she does not move.)* There, get up, Judy, my dear; I won't hit you any more. None of your shamming. This is only your fun. Have you got a headache? Why, you're only asleep. Get up I say. Ah, well, then get down. *(tosses the body down with the end of his stick).* He, he, he! *(Punch sings...)*

Who'd be plagued with a wife
That could set himself free
With a rope or a knife,
Or a good stick like me?

Enter Pretty Polly.

PUNCH. *(seeing her and singing while she dances)*
When the heart of a man is oppressed with cares,
The clouds are dispelled when a woman appears...etc
   PUNCH. *(aside)* What a beauty! What a pretty creature! *(She
continues to dance, and dances round him while Punch watches her
in silent delight. He then begins to sing a slow tune and dances with
her; as the music quickens, they jig backwards , and forwards, then
sideways and to all parts of the stage. At last Punch catches the
lady in his arms and kisses her most loudly, while she appears to
have no objection. After dancing together again, Punch sings as
follows:*

I love you so, I love you so,
I never will leave you; no, no, no!

Curtain closes slowly.

ACT II

*Enter a figure dressed like a courtier, who sings a slow air and
moves to it with great solemnity. He first takes off his hat on the
right side and then on the left, and carries it in his hand. He then
stops in the centre; the music ceases and suddenly his throat begins
to stretch and his head gradually rises until his neck is taller than
the rest of his body. After pausing for some time, the head sinks
again and, as soon as it has come down to its natural place, the
figure disappears. Enter Punch from behind the curtain, where he
had been watching the movements of the strange figure.*
   PUNCH. Who on earth are you, I should like to know, with
your long neck? You may get it stretched for you one of these days,
by somebody else. It's a very fine day. *(Peeping out and looking
up at the sky)* I'll go fetch my horse and take a ride to see my pretty
Poll. *(He sings to the tune of "Sally in our Alley":)*

Of all the girls that are so smart,
There's none like Pretty Polly;

She is the darling of my heart,
She is so gay and jolly.
(Exit singing...)

Re-enter Punch leading his horse by the bridle over his arm. It prances about, and seems very unruly.

PUNCH. Wo, ho! My fine fellow! Wo, ho! Hector! Stand still can't you, and let me get my foot up to the stirrup?

(While Punch is trying to mount, the horse runs away round the stage and Punch sets off after him, catches him by the tail and so stops him. Punch then mounts by sitting on the front of the stage and with both hands lifting one of his legs over the animals back. At first it goes pretty steadily, but soon quickens its pace; while Punch, who does not keep his seat very well, cries "Wo, ho! Hector, ho, ho!" but to no purpose, for the horse sets off at full gallop jerking Punch at every stride with great violence. Punch lays hold round the neck, but is presently thrown upon the platform.)

PUNCH. Oh, dear! Help! Help! I am murdered! I'm a dead man! Will nobody save my life? Doctor! Come and bring me to life again! I'm a dead man! Doctor! Doctor! Doctor!

DOCTOR. Who calls so loud?

PUNCH. Oh, dear! Oh, dear! Murder!

DOCTOR. What is the matter? Bless me! Who is this? My good friend Mr. Punch? Have you had an accident, or are you only taking a nap on the grass after dinner?

PUNCH. Oh, Doctor! Doctor! I have been thrown from my horse. I have been killed!

DOCTOR. No, no, Mr. Punch; you're not so bad as that, sir; you are not killed.

PUNCH. Not dead, but speechless! Oh, Doctor! Doctor!

DOCTOR. Where are you hurt? Is it here? *(touching his head)*

PUNCH. No; lower.

DOCTOR. Here? *(touching his chest.)*

PUNCH. No; lower still.

DOCTOR. Then is your handsome leg broken? *(as the doctor*

G·Cᵏ

leans over Punch's legs to examine them, Punch kicks him in the eye.)

DOCTOR. Oh, my eye! My eye! *(exit the Doctor)*

PUNCH. *(to himself)* Aye, you're right enough; it is all my eye! *(jumping up and singing:)*

> The Doctor is surely an ass, sirs,
> To think I'm as brittle as glass, sirs;
> But I only fell down on the grass sirs,
> And my hurt - it is all my eye!

(While Punch is singing and dancing the Doctor enters behind and hits Punch several times on the head. Punch shakes his ears.)

PUNCH. Hullo! Hullo! Doctor, what game are you up to now? Have you done! What have you got there?

DOCTOR. Physic, Mr. Punch. *(hits him)* Physic for you.

PUNCH. I don't like physic; it give me one big headache.

DOCTOR. That's because you do not take enough of it *(hits him again.)* The more you take, the more good it will do you *(Hits him.)*

PUNCH. So you Doctors always say. Try how you like it yourself.

DOCTOR. We never take our own physic if we can help it. *(Hits him.)* A little more, Mr. Punch, and you will soon be well. *(Hits him.)*

(During this part of the dialogue the Doctor hunts Punch from place to place and at last gets him into a corner and belabours him until Punch is almost stunned.)

PUNCH. Oh, Doctor! Doctor! No more, no more! Enough pyshic for me! I am quite well now!

DOCTOR. Only another dose. *(Hits him.)*

PUNCH. No more! Turn and turn about is all fair, you know. *(Punch makes a desperate effort, wrestles with the Doctor, and after a struggle succeeds in getting the stick away from him.)* Now Doctor, it's your turn to be physicked. *(Beating the Doctor.)*

DOCTOR. Hold, Mr. Punch! I don't want any physic, my

good sir.

PUNCH. Oh yes, you do; you're very bad - you must take it! I am the Doctor now. *(Hits him.)* How do you like physic? *(Hits.)* It will do you good. *(Hits.)* This will soon cure you. *(Hits.)* Physic! *(Hits.)* Physic! *(Hits.)* Physic! *(Hits.)*

DOCTOR. Oh, pray Mr. Punch, no more! One pill of that physic is a dose!

PUNCH. Doctors always die when they take there own physic. *(Hits him.)* Another small dose and you will never want physic again. *(Hits him.)* There, don't you feel the physic in your inside? *(Punch thrusts the end of the stick into the Doctors stomach, the Doctor falls down dead, and Punch as before tosses away the body with the end of his staff.)* He! He! He! *(Laughing.)* Now Doctor, you may cure yourself, if you can. *(Sing's and dances to the tune of "Green grow the rashes, O!")*

> Right toll de riddle doll,
> There's an end of him, old goll!
> I'll dance and sing
> Like anything
> With music for my pretty Poll.

(Exit and re-enter Punch with a large sheep-bell, which he rings violently, dancing about the while, shaking the bell and his head at the same time, and singing a song, beginning "Mr. Punch is a very fine man". Enter a servant in a foreign livery.)

SERVANT. Mr. Punch, my master he say he no like dat noise.

PUNCH. *(with surprise and mocking the servant.)* Your master, he say he no like dat noise! What noise!

SERVANT. Dat nasty noise.

PUNCH. Do you call music a noise?

SERVANT. My master he no like de music, Mr. Punch, so he'll have no more noise near his house.

PUNCH. He, don't don't he? Very well. *(Punch runs about ringing his bell as loudly as he can.)*

SERVANT. Get away, I say, wid dat nasty bell.

PUNCH. What bell?

SERVANT. That bell. *(striking it with his hand.)*

PUNCH. That's a good one! Do you call this a bell? *(Patting it.)* It is an organ.

SERVANT. I say it is a bell, a nasty bell.

PUNCH. I say it is an organ. *(striking him with it.)* What do you say it is now?

SERVANT. An organ, Mr. Punch.

PUNCH. An organ? I say it is a fiddle. Can't you see? *(Offers to strike him again.)*

SERVANT. It is a fiddle.

PUNCH. I say it is a drum.

SERVANT. It is a drum, Mr. Punch.

PUNCH. I say it is a trumpet.

SERVANT. Well, so it is a trumpet. But bell, organ, fiddle, drum or trumpet my master he say he no like de music.

PUNCH. Then bell, organ, fiddle, drum or trumpet, Mr. Punch he say your master is a fool!

SERVANT. And he say, too, he will not have it near his house.

PUNCH. He's a fool, I say, not to like my sweet music! Tell him so - be off! *(hits him with the bell.)* Get along! *(Driving the servant round the place backwards and striking him often with the bell.)* Be off! Be off! *(Knocking him off the platform. Exit Servant. Punch continues to ring the bell as loudly as before, while he sings and dances.)*

Re-enter Servant, slily with a stick. Punch, perceiving him, retreats behind the side curtain, and remains upon the watch. The servant does the same, but leaves the end of the stick visible. Punch again comes forward, sets down his bell very gently, and creeps across the stage, marking his steps with his hands upon the platform, to ascertain whereabouts his enemy is. He then returns to his bell, takes it up, and going quietly over the stage, hits the servant a heavy blow through the curtain, and retires, ringing his bell on the opposite side.

SERVANT. You one nasty, noisy, impudent rascal! Me catch you yet. *(hides again, as before.)*

Enter Punch and strikes him, as before, with the bell. The servant pops out and aims a blow, but not quickly enough to hit Punch who disappears.

SERVANT. You scoundrel, rascal, thief, vagabond, and liar! You shall pay for this, depend upon it!

He stands back. Enter Punch with his bell, who seeing the Servant with his stick retreats instantly and returns also armed with a staff, which he does not at first show. The servant comes forward and strikes Punch on the head so hard a blow that it seems to confuse him.

SERVANT. Me teach you how to ring you nasty, noisy bell near de gentilmen's houses.

PUNCH. *(recovering)* Two can play at that game!

He hits the servant with his stick. A conflict. After a long struggle, during which the combatants exchange sticks and perform various manoeuvres, Punch gains the victory and knocks the enemy down on the platform by repeated blows on the head.)

SERVANT. Oh, dear! Oh, my head!

PUNCH. And, oh your tail too! How do you like that, and that, and that? *(Hitting him each time.)* Do you like that music better than the other? This is my bell *(hits)*, this my organ *(hits)* this my fiddle *(hits)*, this my drum *(hits)*, and this my trumpet *(hits)* - there! A whole concert for you!

SERVANT. No more! Me dead!

PUNCH. Quite dead?

SERVANT. Yes, quite!

PUNCH. Then there's the last for luck! *(Hits him and kills him. He then takes hold of the body by its legs, swings it round two or three times, and throws it away.)*

ACT III

Enter an old Blind Man, feeling his way with a staff. He goes to the opposite side where he knocks.

BLIND MAN. Poor blind man, Mr. Punch; I hope you'll bestow your charity. I hear that you are very good and kind to the poor, Mr. Punch. Pray have pity upon me, and may you never know

the loss of your tender eyes! *(Listens, putting his ear to the side, and, hearing nobody coming, knocks again.)* I lost my sight by the sands in Egypt - poor blind man. Pray, Mr. Punch, have compassion upon the poor blind. *(Coughs)* Only a halfpenny to buy something for my bad cough - only one halfpenny *(knocks again)*.

Punch enters and receives one of the knocks intended for the door upon his head.

PUNCH. Hullo, you old blind rascal! Can't you see?

BLIND MAN. No, Mr. Punch. Pray, sir, bestow your charity upon a poor blind man with a bad cough *(coughs)*.

PUNCH. Get along, get along! Don't trouble me! Nothing for you. Get away! *(Seizes the Blind Man's staff and knocks him off the stage. Punch hums a tune, and dances it, and then begins to sing, in the mock Italian style, the following words, pretending to play the fiddle on his arm with the stick;)*

When I think on you, my jewel,
Wonder not my heart is sad;
You're so fair; and yet so cruel,
You're enough to drive me mad.
On thy lover take some pity,
And relieve this bitter smart.
Think you, Heaven has made you pretty
But to break your lover's heart?

Enter a Constable.

CONSTABLE. Leave off your singing, Mr. Punch, for I'm come to make you sing on the wrong side of your mouth.

PUNCH. Why, who are you?

CONSTABLE. Don't you know me?

PUNCH. No, and don't want to know you.

CONSTABLE. Oh, but you must; I am the constable.

PUNCH. And who sent for you?

CONSTABLE. I'm sent for you.

PUNCH. I don't want a constable. I can settle my own business without a constable, I thank you. I don't want a constable.

CONSTABLE. But the constable wants you.

PUNCH. Oh, does he! What for pray?

CONSTABLE. You killed Mr. Scaramouch. You knocked his head off his shoulders.

PUNCH. What's that to you? If you stay here much longer I'll serve you the same.

CONSTABLE. Don't tell me! You have committed murder, and I've a warrant for your arrest.

PUNCH. And I've a warrant for you. *(Punch knocks him down, and dances and sings about eh stage to tune of "Green grow the rashes, O!")*

Enter an Officer, in a cocked hat with a cockade, and a long pigtail.

OFFICER. Stop your noise, my fine fellow.

PUNCH. Sha'n't!

OFFICER. I'm an officer.

PUNCH. Very well. Did I say you were not?

OFFICER. You must go with me. You killed your wife and child.

PUNCH. They were my own, I suppose; and I had a right to do what I like with them.

OFFICER. We shall see about that; I've come to take you up.

PUNCH. And I'm come to take you down! *(Punch knocks his down, and sings and dances as before.)*

Enter Jack Ketch, in a fur cap. Punch, while dancing, runs up against him without seeing him.

PUNCH. (with some signs of alarm) My dear sir, I beg you one thousand pardons - very sorry.

JACK KETCH. Aye, you'll be sorry enough before I've done with you. Don't you know me?

PUNCH. Oh, sir, I know you very well, and I hope you are very well, and Mrs. Ketch is very well.

JACK KETCH. Mr. Punch, you're a very bad man. Why did you kill the Doctor?

PUNCH. In self defence.

JACK KETCH. That won't do.

PUNCH. He wanted to kill me.

JACK KETCH. How?

PUNCH. With his horrid physic.

. *JACK KETCH.* That's all gammon! You must come to prison - my name's Ketch.

PUNCH. Ketch this then! *(punch knocks down Jack Ketch, and continues to dance and sing.)*

Enter behind, one after the other, the Constable, the Officer and Jack Ketch. They fall upon Punch in the order in which they enter, and after a noisy struggle, they pin him in a corner and finally carry him off while he loudly calls out "Help! Murder!" etc.

The curtain at the back of the stage rises, and discovers Punch in prison, rubbing his nose against the bars and poking it through them.

PUNCH. Oh, dear! Oh, dear! What will become of poor pill-garlick now? My pretty Poll, when shall I see you again? *(Sings to the air of "Water parted from the sea";)*

> Punch, when parted from his dear,
> Still must ring in doleful tune.
> I wish I had those rascals here,
> I'd settle all their hashes soon.

Enter Jack Ketch. He fixes a gibbet on the platform of the stage, and then retires.

PUNCH. Well, I declare now, that's very pretty. That must be a gardener. What a handsome tree he has planted just opposite the window, and what a fine view of the country!

Enter the Constable. He places a ladder next to the gibbet then retire.

PUNCH. Stop thief! Stop thief! There's one pretty rascal for you! He'll come back again and get up the ladder to steal the fruit out of the tree.

Enter two men with a coffin. They set it down on the platform and retire.

PUNCH. What's that for, I wonder? Oh, dear! I see now.

G.6ᵉ

What a fool I was! This is a large basket to put the fruit into!

Re-enter Jack Ketch.

JACK KETCH. Now Mr. Punch, you may come out, if you like it.

PUNCH. Thank you, kindly; but I am very well where I am. This is a very nice place, with a pretty view of the country.

JACK KETCH. What! Won't you come out, and have a good dinner for nothing?

PUNCH. Much obliged, Mr. Ketch, but I have had my dinner for nothing already.

JACK KETCH. Then a good supper?

PUNCH. I never eat suppers; they are not wholesome.

JACK KETCH. But you must come out. Come out and be hanged.

PUNCH. You would not be so cruel.

JACK KETCH. Why were you so cruel as to commit so many murders?

PUNCH. But that's no reason why you should be cruel, too, and murder me.

JACK KETCH. Come out, immediately!

PUNCH. I can't; I've got a bone in my leg.

JACK KETCH. And you've got one bone in your neck, but that shall soon be broken. Well, then, I must fetch you. *(he goes to the prison, and after a struggle, in which Punch calls out, "Mercy! Mercy! I'll never do so again!" Jack Ketch brings him out to the front of stage.)*

PUNCH. Oh dear! Oh dear! Be quiet! Can't you let me be?

JACK KETCH. Now, Mr. Punch, no more delay. Put your head through this loop.

PUNCH. Through there? What for?

JACK KETCH. Yes, through there.

PUNCH. What for? I don't know how.

JACK KETCH. It is very easy - only put your head through here.

PUNCH. What! - So! *(poking his head on one side of the noose.)*

JACK KETCH. No, no, here!

PUNCH. So, then? *(Poking his head on the other side.)*

JACK KETCH. Not so, you idiot!

PUNCH. Mind how you call me names. Try if you can to do it yourself. Only show me how and I'll do it directly.

JACK KETCH. Very well, I will. There, you see my head and you see this loop - put it in so. *(Putting his head through the noose.)*

PUNCH. And pull it tight so. *(He pulls the body down with a jerk and hangs Jack Ketch.)* Hurrah! Hurrah! *(Punch takes down the corpse and places it in the coffin; he then stands back. Enter two men, who remove the gibbet, and placing the coffin upon it, dance with it on their shoulders grotesquely and retire.)*

PUNCH. There they go. They think they have got Mr. Punch safe enough. *(Sings:)*

> They're out! They're out! I've done the trick!
> Jack Ketch is dead - I'm free;
> I do not care now if Old Nick
> Himself should come for me.

ACT IV

Enter Punch, with a stick. He dances about, beating time on the front of the stage, and singing to the tune of "Green Grow the Rashes, O!"

> Right foll de riddle loll,
> I'm the boy to do them all;
> Here's a stick
> To trash Old Nick,
> If he by chance upon me call.

Enter the Devil. He peeps in at the corner of the stage, and retires. Devil.

PUNCH. (Much frightened, and retreating as far he can) Oh dear! Oh dear! Talk of the Devil, and he pops up his horns. There

the old gentleman is, sure enough. *(A pause and dead silence, while Punch continues to gaze at the spot where the devil appeared. The Devil comes forward.)* Good, kind Mr. Devil, I never did you any harm, but all the good in my power. There, don't come any nearer. How do you do, sir? *(Plucking up courage.)* I hope you and all your family are very well? Much obliged for this visit. Good morning. Should be sorry to keep you, for I know you have a great deal of business when you come to London. *(The Devil comes nearer.)* Oh dear! What will become of me? *(The Devil springs at Punch, who escapes, and aims a blow at his enemy; the Devil eludes it, as well as many others, laying his head on the platform, and moving it rapidly backwards and forwards, so that Punch, instead of striking him, only hits the boards. Exit the Devil.)*

PUNCH. He! He! He! *(Laughing)* He's off! He knew which side his bread was buttered on. He's very cunning. *(Punch is here alarmed by hearing a strange and unearthly whirring noise, something like the rapid motion of fifty spinning wheels, and again retreats to the corner, fearfully awaiting the event.)*
Re-enter the Devil, with a stick. He makes up to Punch, who retreats round the back of the stage, and they stands eying one another and fencing at opposite ides. At last the Devil aims a straight blow at Punch, which falls on the back of his head.

PUNCH. Oh, my head! What is that for? Pray Mr. Devil, let us be friends. *(The Devil hits him again, and Punch begins to grow angry.)* Why, you must be one very stupid Devil not to know your best friend when you see him. *(The Devil hits him again.)* Be quiet, I say, you hurt me! Well, if you won't, we must see who is the best man - Punch or the Devil.
(Here commences a terrific struggle between the Devil and Punch. In the beginning Punch has much the worst of it, being hit by his black enemy when and where he pleases. At last, the Devil seems to grow weary and Punch succeeds in planting several heavy blows. The balance being restored, the fight is kept up for some time, and towards the end, Punch has the decided advantage, and drives his enemy before him. The Devil is at length stunned by repeated blows on the head and horns, and falls forward on the platform, where

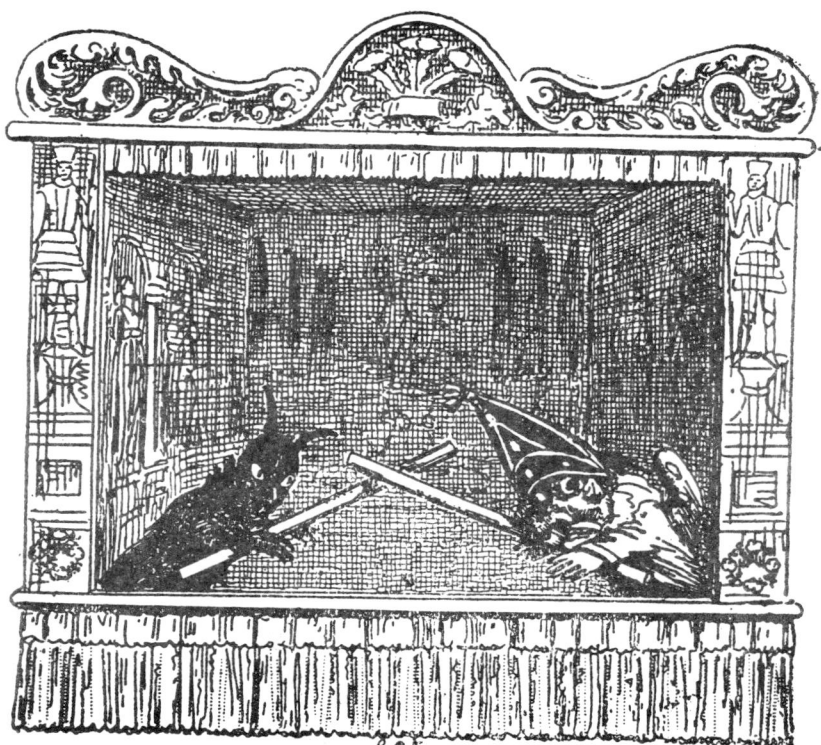

Punch completes his victory, and knocks the breath out of his body
Punch then sticks his staff into the Devil's body and whirls him
round in the air, exclaiming;

Hurrah, Hurrah the Devil's dead!
You can all go home safely and sleep sound in your bed,
The Devil with mighty a blow is eluded,
So now it's goodnight for this tale is concluded.